White Shade

A Real-World Primer for the Black Professional Woman

Dr. Michelle L. Shelton

CONTENTS

FOREWORD

This text is an encapsulation of different experiences shared with me, and has been fictionalized in an effort to build a storyline around the snapshotted narratives I have come across in my walk through life.

White Shade: A Real-World Primer for the Black Professional Woman intends to serve as a proverbial compass for all individuals: leaders, aspiring leaders, white people, Black people, and all other people, but specifically aims to empower aspiring Black, professional, educated women to understand and out-maneuver some of the social obstacles of the "white space" they will likely face in their respective industries.

Overall, the intent of this text is to help us to see ourselves, to judge ourselves, and to evaluate our decisions through the lenses of semi-fictional characters. It is through these unique lenses that can teach us to navigate our humanity as leaders within our households, within our places of work, and within our other respective social networks. *White Shade: A Real-World Primer for the Black Professional Woman* informs us that Black women must be psychologically resilient in order to fully operate and in order to fully thrive within the dominant culture this is coined the "white space".

This text also informs us that our decisions have very real consequences on the social well-being of others, and it is my hope that this text will allow readers to dig for a sense of empathy and connectivity, which is necessary to arrive at our intended humanity.

DEDICATION

This book is dedicated to my mother, Brenda Long and my father, Vincent Shelton. If it had not been for their individual experiences, they would not have found it necessary to share with me their pains and triumphs. For this, I am proud, because it is what shaped me into the woman I have become.

I must also acknowledge my sisters, LaShonda (Shonda), Bernadette (Bern), and Christina (Chrissy), who have each created their own path inspired by the life lessons they each have encountered. As a result, they are the very best models of Black, professional, educated women. I am proud and blessed that they have mentored me throughout my journey – even still. They have each in their own way set the blueprint for my life, and I am so grateful.

Thank you for planting me, watering me, and giving me light.

INTRODUCTION

So, What?

White Shade is found in what is called the "white space"

Throughout history, Black women have found themselves at the metaphorical frontline of the insufferable inequality that she and her male counterpart had to and still endure. As daughter, wife, and mother, she has witnessed, and she has persisted through the racial mistreatment with an uprightness that should have been tainted as a result of the psychological and physical

1

oppressions she and her father, husband, and son had to endure.

However, she, a woman, not only has been predisposed to the mistreatment of Black people, she has also withstood the test of living as a woman, which comes with its own injustices. Society perceives women as the weaker between sexes, and society also denotes Blackness to equate as the inferior of races.

Harvard Kennedy School's Women and Public Policy Program published a review which discusses the "double jeopardy" Black women experience. The review reports that, "Since Black women are members of two marginalized groups (Black and female), they might experience greater discrimination, a 'double jeopardy', compared to the discrimination faced by individuals that hold one marginalized identity (i.e. white women or Black men)," and the review goes on to state, "Biases about race and gender could impact judgments of how much a leader is given credit

2

for organizational success or judged harshly for organizational failure."

Nonetheless, Black women continue to stand at the frontline for her race through her educational and professional endurance. Samuel Osborne, an international and national reporter writes that, "By both race and gender, a higher percentage of black women (9.7%) is enrolled in college than any other group, including Asian women (8.7%), white women (7.1%) and white men (6.1%). However, a recent study found Black women make up just (8%) of private sector jobs and (1.5%) of leadership roles.

According to the *Institute for Women's Policy Research*, "Black women won't receive full pay equality compared to white men until the year 2119, if we continue to make progress at the current pace. That's [nearly] one hundred years away from today. For purposes of comparison, white women will receive pay equity to white men in the year 2055."

Sonia Johnson, a Consultant, a Public Speaker, and a Business Owner further notes, "Combine making less money for doing the same job, with the many documented slights Black women encounter on a daily basis while working in corporate environments, it isn't surprising to see that so many of them flee the world of employment to become their own boss."

Within professional institutions all over the country and all over the world, the Black woman faces shrewd attempts to minimize her contribution and to discredit her value. Such degradation is because of her race *coupled* with her sex, and in these environments, it is done in the most subliminal way possible – in a way that is enveloped in passive nuances of psychology. However, if she does not understand the attempts, and if she does not regulate them accordingly, it is designed for her intended end.

In January 2020, *Forbes* published an article titled,
"Recognizing Workplace Challenges Faced by Black Women
Leaders," the author writes:

> The *American Bar Association* found that Black
> women are often excluded from their firms'
> internal networks, seldom offered opportunities
> for client contact, and infrequently receive
> challenging assignments. Indeed, 66 percent of
> Black women were found to have been excluded
> from both formal and informal networking
> opportunities, but only six percent of white
> women had been. Black women's experiences in
> other professions and business arenas are no
> different from their experiences in law.

The Black colloquialism "to throw shade" means to insult or
to trash talk someone. Additionally, the "white space" has a
multitude of meanings. However, in this text, you will come
to know that "white space" means an arena created by,

designated for, and operated by white people. This space proves to be advantageous and familiar for white people, while it concurrently proves to be disadvantageous and unfamiliar for Black people. In these spaces, Black people, women in particular, must come to know and become savvy with "white shade", which in essence are white society's subtle and passive aggressive methods to marginalize Black people – in this case, Black women in educational and professional settings. These settings are the "white space".

Therefore, as a Black, professional, educated woman, I must speak the truth as I know it through my experience and the experience of other Black, professional, educated women. As a result of my own ignorance with politics, which comprises the "white space", I have made some missteps like so many of my colleagues have. *White Shade: A Real-World Primer for the Black Professional Woman* intends to serve as a guide for those young Black women going into higher education or into the professional arena, which is the "white space" full of "white shade", while concurrently validating the experience of so many seasoned Black, professional, educated women. This primer is also a reflection tool for those experienced Black, professional, educated woman, who are presently and have already been standing on the frontline for some time.

It is my desire that Black women all over the globe come to an awareness and to an understanding of the characteristics of these spaces, which is why you will read seemingly real, but fictionalized stories of women that encounter "white shade" in the "white space". You will see some of them succeed and some of them fail, but after each vignette, I will offer "A Word of Advice" to prepare you for situations that have or may arise in your experience.

I really hope you enjoy *White Shade: A Real-World Primer for the Black Professional Woman.*

PART 1

Whiting Out the "White Spaces"

CHAPTER 1

I Can Feel My Skin

The untold truth of the happy Black woman

I t is the gentle jingle of my morning alarm that awakens me. Oftentimes, I let the second or third alarm take me out of the bed. I subscribe to The Admiral's philosophy to start the day with an accomplishment, so I begin to make my bed with meticulous care. I step back, and I admire the bed that is situated in a homey space that I have created for myself. *That's* the single me.

The married me wakes up 30 minutes after my husband, who is already out of the shower and applying his lotion with a certain level of carelessness for the task or maybe this is the most crucial part of his routine, but he rhythmically slaps it on and begins to spread it all over his body – seemingly all at once. Though I am vaguely aware of what he's doing, I still rely on the gentle jingle of my morning alarm to awaken me further.

Like the single me, the married me still subscribes to The Admiral's philosophy, so like my single-self, I make our bed with meticulous care, and like the single-me still, I step back to admire the bed that is situated in this magical space that I have created, but we, my husband and I invested in for our romance.

The single and married me enjoy the bliss of showering, because it is my time with my spiritual self. I stand – paying ever so close, but distant and seamless attention to the echoic sound of the innumerous droplets of water from the shower head, and I enjoy the soapy suds that saturate my body. I lather my hair with shampoo; all while imagining the details of the coming day. This is what the single-me and the married-me do.

The married me with children, wakes up 15 minutes before the kids, so I can have this time to myself; it is the 10-minute shower that gives me the rejuvenation I need to face my children and my day, so I grab my robe and I enter my eldest child's room, I kneel beside his bed, and I whisper into his ear, "Ok Honey. You've got to get up, My Love." He sleepily squirms underneath his sheets, and after another soft prompting, he rises from his bed; he wraps his little arms around my waist, and he hugs me just before going into his bathroom to brush his teeth and start his routine.

Feeling blessed, I then go back into my bedroom, and I do my hair and my makeup; as I pass through the hallway to make my way to the baby's room, like clockwork, I know that my husband will be sitting in his suit at the office desk, drinking his coffee, and reading his emails as he waits for our son to finish his routine. After which, he will take our son to school, while on his way to work.

Across from the office is the baby girl's room, and she has a great sense for time, because she is already squirming and making grunting sounds to rise for the morning. I pull her from her crib, and I put my nose to her neck to smell the sweet baby smell she wears effortless. I take her to our bathroom, and I begin to get her ready for her day. By the time I finish giving her a baby bath, my husband enters the bathroom; he takes the baby's towel; he takes her from me as he swaddles her in it, and he kisses her.

As I take her back, he snuggles a kiss in on my neck, and he grabs me near for a hug that only newlyweds and the two of us do. Our son enters and gives me a hug, and I lean down about a foot to kiss him at the bridge of his nose. As the two leave, my husband says, "I'll see you this evening, My Love," and my son says, "Bye Mommy! Love you." I get the baby girl dressed, and I put her in the bassinet just before putting on my office clothes, which I had ironed the night before.

The married mother version of myself appreciates my husband for taking my work bag and pocketbook to the car along with packing and taking the baby girl's bag to the car as well; my hero. All that is left for me to do is take the baby girl from the bassinet to the car seat and then to Mema and Poppa's house. After I drop her off at my parent's, I start my commute to the office.

The single me would have completely by-passed all of the family nuances; the single version of myself would have gotten out of the shower, applied lotion to my body, did my hair and my makeup, got dressed, and then headed to work.

My life is normal at home, whether I am the single me, the married me, or the married me with children; no false pretenses. Nothing changes. However, when I enter into the world, there is this invisible fog that impacts the dynamic of my reality. I can feel my skin. Not just the weight of my skin that alerts me that it's there, because I can actually feel it through my senses, but the weight of my skin that alerts me that it's there, because the color of it somehow elicits so much controversy.

I am a Black, professional, educated woman, and I have wondered how normal *is* normal for those without "Black" in front of their title. I am proud of it, and I wear it with honor, but I feel the unjust weight of it.

I often enter spaces, where I am the only Black person, and I am required to pretend that it is normal to be the only one there. I have also entered spaces where I am *among* the only Black person, and if me and the one or two other Black people happen to look for a more natural conversation between the two of us or among the three of us, the room seems to notice, and say, "What are these Black people talking about? Probably some ghetto stuff like affirmative action and food stamps or something." They throw their "white shade", laugh, and continue their normal business.

However, they never encounter spaces where they are not the majority. They never have to make an adjustment. They leave home feeling normal, and they enter into other arenas *still* feeling normal. They will never turn on the television and flip through channels in search of a positive representation of themselves – not because it does not exist, but because it is intentionally undocumented or not advertised. They do not have to worry that they will be misrepresented over and over and over again throughout media.

They do not have to worry about the character assassination that is sure to be executed by media outlets everywhere after an unarmed Black man or child is slain during a routine traffic stop or chance encounter with an overzealous member of the neighborhood watch. The truth of a scholar athlete that maintained a 4.0 GPA all four years of high school and accepted on a full ride – untold. What will the media say?

It is this character assassination that morphs and reduces an Ivy league graduate, a 4.0 scholar and all-star athlete, a family man, or a dutiful son into nothing more than an ill-advised profile picture, social media post or juvenile school record.

They never have to worry about entering a conference room with more degrees than a thermometer, with tremendous research abilities, with amazing leadership and communications skills and be undermined and undervalued despite meticulous work ethic and drive. As I drive to the office each day, I drive there well-aware that I am being undermined and undervalued, because my Black face has the audacity to operate in a "white space".

Nonetheless, every day I get to my office 20 minutes early, so I can sit at my desk to remember my 10-minute shower.

(#)

This first vignette provides a fly-on-the-wall account of so many Black women that are either single, are married, or are married with children. It was written to provide some insight of the untold truth – that a majority of Black women play and desire to play a harmoniously collaborative role with their husband within their household – a collaboration built on peace, which empowers a sacred bond that love gels together.

What Black women do in their household is a spiritual ritual that prepares us for a society that simply does not like us or want to respect us – especially if we are professional and educated.

Additionally, a marketing definition for "white space" is highlighted in this text because the media does not portray the truth of the happy Black single woman, the happy Black married woman, and the happy Black married woman with children nor does it truthfully or fully portray her husband, brother, or son. This vignette captures a writer's definition for "white space," because it encapsulates the truth of the Black woman's experience through creative writing.

Lastly, a third definition of "white space" is unraveled through a societal connotation; this story sheds light on the white privilege that has been normalized outside of a Black household; it can be paralyzing to Black women – especially, because despite the effects, she must overcome the blatant disregard of her very existence, and so it has become her daily practice to tap deep into her spiritual-self to seek refuge.

A Word of Advice

Before becoming engulfed in the "white space", take time to meditate (or to pray) yourself into a frame of mind that is ready for whatever challenges you might be confronted with that day.

Like the main character in the first vignette, some may find the shower to be their place of spiritual connectedness, and experience the literal act of cleaning as a symbol of spiritual cleansing. While showering may be natural for some to get into a state of passive meditation, others might treat their commute to and from work as a silent prayer that brings their thoughts back to a place of balance and tranquility.

Another might wake up 20 minutes earlier than the rest of her household, so she can warm up a kettle until it softly screams, and then pour its contents into a cup over sugar and a teabag; she might sit at the dining room table tasting every grainy flavor of warm herbs. This is her secret place of meditative silence.

Whatever you do, please be intentional about appreciating these moments, so when the day gets going, you can draw from it whenever you need it.

CHAPTER 2

A Seat at the Table

Which one are you?

The table is representative of the parliamentary-like expectations governed by the "white space". This proverbial table has been set in such an intentional manner over many generations, and Black, professional, educated women often have access to it. However, when there is more than one of them at the table, there is this magnetic repellent that signifies that their similarities cannot bond to one another.

If there is any rapport among them, no one would ever know. So, when they have this disjointed seat at the table, there are several characters you will surely find among a sea of "white space".

<u>(#)</u>

Ms. Uneasy is new to the organization, but she somehow can feel the essence of her new environment; that being the air of superiority seeping out of the ventilation system. She notices its breeze travels from one office space to the next and through the hallways. She cannot understand how a breeze such as this has the power to maneuver in phone conversations, emails, and within dialogues during small conferences. She suspects that there is some kind of contagious epidemic going around.

It has to be clear to everyone that even if Ms. Uneasy is not new to the company, which she is, she is at least new to the department, but the fact that they do not seem to notice is starting to make her feel irrelevant. Additionally, she looks all around her and can clearly see that she is the only Black woman in the department. Not-to-mention her mocha skin and healthy size are delicacies in a place of vanilla, olive, and twig. But, all the same, she receives nothing more than a new office space.

Within the first few days of her starting, a couple of 5-years-removed from college employees stops by to say, "Welcome," and two of the more seasoned assistants stop by her office to welcome her with a pastry and orange juice from the cafeteria. Now a week in, she has this repetitive thought of how insignificant her presence and work is within this organization. She thinks to herself, "As one of the Seniors in the organization, I wonder how they welcome other new employees?"

Word has it, in the recent past, the department would reserve a private room at one of the area restaurants to host a welcome luncheon as an opportunity for the team to meet-and-greet the new Senior or Director or Executive. Now, the department has been strong-arming the excuse that there have been budget cuts, and coincidentally Ms. Uneasy is the first beneficiary to this new concept of a funding dessert.

Early one morning, Ms. Uneasy is standing in front of the *Keurig* making a cup of coffee to jumpstart her day, and one of the Directors, Mr. So-and-So enters just as she is pouring the liquid into her coffee mug; he does not say, "Hello." He walks over to the microwave, and takes off the lid of his container; he places the container inside, and then begins a button-beeping frenzy in an attempt to set it to the desired time.

Ms. Uneasy, says, "Hello," as she takes in a great heap of air for a yawn. Mr. So-and-So says as if to be inconvenienced, "Good morning," and he simultaneously takes in a great heap of air for a yawn as well. Ms. Uneasy instantly thinks about the blog she had read about a month ago. She recalls the author of it expressing a sense of boredom regarding the recent political commentary. The author wrote, "I often pinch myself to make sure I stay awake – yawn *[sic]* better yet, alive with the mumbo jumbo that takes center stage among more penetrating topics."

Ms. Uneasy laughs to herself, because for some odd reason, the not so crafty image the author had created in the blog helped her to visualize the author yawning. And as a result, she remembers yawning as she read the author's words. For some reason, this morning as she thinks of the air of superiority that penetrates space and time in this place, as she pours her coffee into her mug, and as she says, "Hello" to arrest the inhumanity of this moment; it is her having taken in a great heap of air that somehow manages to stimulate a contagious empathy from an unexpected source.

Moments later, she takes her mug and heads out of the staff lounge. Once she gets back to her office, her phone rings, and she sees the name of one of the supervisors from another department showing up on her caller ID. She answers, but the caller does not realize that she is on the line, and Ms. Uneasy can hear what sounds like the caller taking in a great heaping breathe, which then causes Ms. Uneasy to pull away the phone so as not to be heard as she lets out a yawn. With a breathy, "I'm sorry," the caller says, "I haven't yet had my morning coffee. Forgive me." Ms. Uneasy hearing a voice that sounds much like her brother or her father on the other end says, "No worries, but I have to admit, even though I have mine in hand, it hasn't kicked in yet, because you've just made me yawn too."

They both laugh, and he introduces himself and then congratulates her for beating out 3 rounds of a total of 24 of the company's top candidates, and he welcomes her to the company. After Ms. Uneasy gets off of the phone, she realizes exactly what is at play here. Just like the psychology behind the contagion of an empathetic yawn, there is this plague of competitive title-based superiority – a passive aggressive attempt at wrestling colleagues into submission.

As a result, when Ms. Uneasy sits in on conferences – small or large, and though she takes a back seat, her participation is wrapped up in nervous energy, because she is not clear as to who has been affected nor is she sure of if there is a game of cunning trickery tied to this contagious air that members of this environment are breathing.

(#)

Mrs. Arrogant was raised in the South Side of Chicago; however, her parents kept her sheltered. So, at the time, her experience with urban underprivileged populations was more like looking down upon them from her high tower. She had been groomed into not mingling with them, and she understood that she was only to associate with those who were also sitting high and behind the metaphorical palace walls and looking low into the valleys. Consequently, there were few Black girls living near the castle; they lived in the valley, so all of her friends were white or white-Latinas.

She would not even notice if she tried, but as a teenager and young adult she talked to these friends in a way that further distanced herself from associating with any other girl that may have looked like the image of herself – kinky hair, weaved hair, braided hair, or permed hair with brown skin, because she assumed that their experience was one of an urban underprivileged lineage. A lineage she had been so far removed from, and so the mere association with it was unattractive and uninteresting to her.

The irony is that she left home to attend a historically Black college. The logic was to further explore the great contributors to her culture; however, her connectedness to the struggles of the great contributors had been amiss, because she could not see how struggle had been the catalyst to their greatness.

On a social level, she had silently admired the Black female Greeks who strolled and stomped the yard, but she did not imagine stepping down from her philosophical heights to approach them or anyone that seemed to embrace the entire essence of the culture. A culture saturated with rising out of the pitfalls of societal conditioning and into the wonders of living as creative pioneers of modern culture. Mrs. Arrogant convinced herself that she only was attracted to and interested in a façade.

Since her experience was that of a hypothetical Greek big sister called High and Mighty, she did not recognize that the only person she would spend her time was with her high-achieving scholar athlete boyfriend, who recognized that he was dating a woman that was living an unimpressive, superficial, and lonely college experience. Though he loved her, he hated this about her, and so he slept with other women behind her back.

Yet she never caught him, she could sense it, because the looks she would get from beautiful shades of brown women would trigger her female intuition. Nevertheless, she remained with him; with him she spent every second she could squeeze out of him. Eventually, he felt like *he* was suffocating; he wanted time with his football buddies, and he wanted time with his girl on the side – Redbone with the ginger kinky hair and slender frame, so he said to his girlfriend who would later become his wife, "You really have to find something else to do other than to be with me."

Years later, they married, and as he elevated himself, she did her best to keep up. Six years into their marriage they had a couple of children, but when their eldest turned 4 and their youngest was 2, he decided it was time to uncover the truth that created a deep and untreated festering sore between the two of them. He slowly, but thoughtfully unveiled the face he had been masquerading for 11 years. He told his wife of his infidelity during their college years, and its resulting child, who is now 10-years-old.

Intuitively, Mrs. Arrogant flashed back to Redbone with the ginger kinky hair and slender frame, and she remembered discerning eye-contact they both shared with one another; she remembered eventually not seeing Redbone around campus anymore, and she remembered rumors of Redbone's pregnancy. He apologized with strong conviction and true remorse, and she stood behind him.

He made partner with his firm, and several years later, she became an Executive in her new company. However, his rise came with great responsibility, so he frequently participated in elite circles of Black excellence. In this lifestyle, Mrs. Arrogant's nerves pulsated in her body, because she thought that she had left this world behind when she had graduated from college.

She dug deep into the bowels of her discomfort, and she found the height upon which she stood looking down on the urban underprivileged population she recollected ignoring as a teenager in her high tower; she remembered that she deemed them unattractive and uninteresting, and for the sake of her husband, she rehearsed false acceptance – the complete opposite of what she was groomed to know. She rehearsed it over and over and over again until she felt she might be convincing to the sea of Black faces that just might entertain her existence out of respect for her husband.

Therefore, today as Mrs. Arrogant sits in her authority as one of the Executives in her company, she is comfortable being, but one among a sea of "white space", and this is her high tower.

(#)

Ms. Confident was the youngest member of her household growing up; she has four sisters and no brothers. She was a carefree child; she was so carefree that she did not realize that school was to be taken seriously, and as a result she had to repeat first grade. Her father who was into self-improvement and psychology text, began to cultivate the mind of a carefree child into one that became more inward thinking and self-actualizing.

His training created a very connected child. At a young age, her peers were drawn to her magic; it was the silent awareness she owned that drew them to her like moths to a fire; though she was the youngest in her family, she was the big sister in her community, in her school, on her sports teams, and eventually in college, and she grew into it in her place of early employment.

Her peers and now constituents would go to her for help to solve problems. From a young age into adulthood, Ms. Confident was self-aware. Overtime, she realized that her life was greater than mere moments, but connected to the lives of others and addressing and supporting their needs.

After having experienced let downs from constituents and superiors with ulterior motives, she learned the hard way that people will not like the person you are just as much as they hate the person you are pretending to be, so she continued to be who she was at all times and in all contexts.

She decided that her sureness in her ability could be attractive or unattractive to others, and she accepted the fact that the attraction lies in the eye of the beholder.

(#)

On the other hand, one of Ms. Confident's sisters, Ms. Strategist was cut from the same cloth, and though she was taught to be confident, her father was at a different place in his life when she was born; he was not yet into self-improvement and self-actualization, but he was learning to play Chess, so when Ms. Strategist was young, he raised her on the game of Chess. He had her imagine the types of moves the pawns, the Knights, the Bishops, the Rooks could make, but he taught her that the Queen's moves are varied and acceptable, because her job is to protect the King, which Ms. Strategist quickly equated to protecting the game itself.

She became an impeccable Chess player as a child, but quickly learned how its philosophy plays out in real life. Once she had made the connection, she began to see people as pieces to a game of Chess.

The beauty is that she never quite managed to see herself as any of the pieces on the board; instead, she saw each piece for what it was; that each move played out to achieve its intended purpose, and she had endless control.

(#)

It is painful to accept the buried realities of so many Black, professional, educated women who are expected to operate with invisibility in the "white space". Black women often struggle with accepting this, because she is typically excellent, so to trim herself to suit the social paradigm might cause her to wear the pain in the form of anxiety like Ms. Uneasy or in denial like Mrs. Arrogant.

However, it is refreshing to know that a majority of Black women fall somewhere between Ms. Confident or Ms.

Strategist. She either will simply own who God has created her to be in the "white space" despite the game of manipulation that is playing out around her or she will be very aware of all the players on the board and interact with them accordingly.

The four stories within this vignette reveal the psychological disenfranchisement of many Black women as a result of the "white space" they are in or have been programmed to think they belong. It concurrently, sheds light on the self-preservation of many Black woman *within* the "white space" despite the hidden political agendas of those who take offense by the presence of Black women within these spaces.

Ms. Uneasy is a character that notices the professional nuances around her and is bothered by the way it makes her feel. However, she is not one that will do anything to improve or worsen conditions. She is afraid of what might happen if she does. Nonetheless, she has been this way her entire life – afraid of conflict, and as a result she often goes unnoticed in most arenas she finds herself.

Ms. Uneasy is one that will address her conflicts in her own conscience or with loved ones, but she will never address those who regularly inflict minor offenses against her. She will work hard and look for favor from her offenders, but find none, and she will wonder why a character like Ms. Strategist gets acknowledgement for being equally effective.

Like her parents, Mrs. Arrogant has only experienced life as the token Black figure, and since she has been indoctrinated to see Black people through a disjointed lens: uneducated, ignorant, unprofessional, inarticulate, and unpolished, Mrs. Arrogant has become the offender. She has embraced the narrative of the "white space" that has been projected upon all Black people. Though, at the unconscious level, she is intuitively aware of her position as the token

Black figure, and she participates within prestigious Black circles to appear what she is not – self-aware.

Her participation in these prestigious Black circles is also meant to serve as talking-points within the "white space" to demonstrate that she should be perceived as the best representation of Black culture. All in all, she suffers from a lack of self-identity, and she is too proud of what she thinks she is to even know it. Unfortunately, those who know her best, exploit her ignorance – like her husband, who wanders off during social events to sop up the culturally conscience conversation of authentically beautiful Black women, who annunciate /t/'s and /s/'s with an air of urban confidence.

On the other hand, Ms. Confident is in her own way naïve, but to some extent, and ironically, she is aware of it. She chalks it up to her faith, but a part of it is the result of her youth and fearlessness. She is not afraid of the consequences, because her inexperience has not yet prepared her for a full understanding of just how severe consequences can be in the "white space".

Knowing her purpose in every arena is why Ms. Confident stays true to who she is through her spiritual connectedness, and her trust in herself. She believes that no matter what, she must remain authentic even in a system that despises who she is. She tells herself that she can handle the consequences that come with truth.

Finally, Ms. Strategist had learned to be observant and analytical – especially as it pertains to people within her circle, because as a child she noticed the interactions between shady adults during the card games and social gatherings her parents would host at their apartment. She would hide in a corner and witness the impact one shady adult would have on another unsuspecting one or even how the perceived mark would in fact be the slickest one of all.

She saw adults as childlike, and she decided adults play more games than children, but she was also shrew enough to realize that adult games have real ramifications and can change the trajectory of someone's life – either favorably or unfavorably. Though she witnessed the cunning nature of adult game play, she chose to embrace the game, to know the game, and to play the game to maintain an advantage in a shady world.

So, as a Black, professional, educated woman in the "white space", she plays the game she learned as a child. She knows the players from the pawns to the royalty; she has observed and analyzed their moves, and she plays whatever piece she is given to her advantage.

A Word of Advice

Internalize the four stories within this vignette so you can see these stories as a self-evaluation tool. Decide which of the four you are? Are you more of one than the others or are you a combination of more than one? Reflect and decide what elements of each character are either going to contribute to their personal failure or their personal success. Determine what each character might need to do to be their best and to experience their most satisfying self.

Pinpoint modifications they may need to make to be both authentic and successful within a "white space".

CHAPTER 3

When We Break Bread Together

Her self-talk of self-doubt in a "white space"

"It's too obvious when we sit together. There are simply too many of us sitting here. How many of us are there? One, two, three...

Okay there is eight of us. Six of us have to disperse and blend in with the other tables. It is only right. *No – no...* I'm not being irrational. What will they think of us?"

As Mrs. Gray speaks these words, she is engrossed in their judgment; she believes her value is incumbent upon their lens. She thinks, "They'll think I do not belong. That can't be. I *do* belong. We simply cannot stay connected like this, because they'll think we're conspiring against them. Ok…ok… I have to be the diplomatic one here. They do not know the cost of their actions. Ok… Since no one else is going to get up, I'm leaving; I'm blending in."

She gets up – uncomfortable with her identity – uncomfortable with us. She gets up, and she readjusts her blouse; she clears her throat, and she puts on her façade. She does this as if she waited her whole entire life for this moment. She does this as her 9-year-old self, who had buried her Kenya doll into the deepest darkest part of her closet, and as if she had just taken her blue-eyed Barbie doll from its wrappings with expectation and with pride.

She walks away from us believing that we had lost our minds. She walks away from us reminding herself that we had gotten it wrong. She walks away wondering how we had forgotten that we are not meant to commune with one another in public – except for church. She thinks to herself, "Church is ok. We can be inclusive at church," and then she remembers, "*And* family reunions? *That* is when it's okay."

Even further away from us, she reassures herself that we definitely should separate at work. "*That*" – she exaggerates the ending *t* "…is where separation is okay." With each step, she takes away from us, her smile broadens, her nostrils flare, and her conscience clears. She believes that her choice is right; that her decision is justified. In her mind, *she* is rational.

Mrs. Gray is not concerned that when we break bread together, we break free of the systematic rut we are so conditioned to take part in. Our drawing to one another is a space that is sacred from the rest of the world. We can reprogram the code to unlock the system, and for a moment, we can get caught up in the abyss of our own familiarity – in our own identity. Mrs. Gray drew herself away from us, because she believed the narrative that was written about her and those that look like her.

Despite sitting among seven other doctoral candidates, looking like her cousins socializing on a dinner break from class, and rather than sit among us, who had embroidered the very fabric to the quilt of her candidacy, she chose to lose out on an opportunity to create a new normal with the rest of us. Instead, she opted to bury us in the deepest darkest part of her closet.

(#)

Mrs. Gray's story is essentially a scenario the character Mrs. Arrogant had experienced. This is why the characters are so similar, because they are the same persona. She is externally a Black woman, but the internal conflict that plagues her mind in this moment reveals that she is struggling with her identity as a Black woman within a "white space", which causes great frustration for her.

45

Her decision reveals that Mrs. Gray refuses to freely own the truth of who she is, and instead of challenging the status quo that is the "white space", she misses out on an opportunity to model the true essence of Black excellence for others to witness; she instead attempts to blend into a "white space". However, since she will always be externally Black – the "white space" sees her as gray, and so do we.

A Word of Advice

As Black women in professional settings, we must seek out opportunities to publicly and professionally confer with one another, because it begins to normalize our noteworthy collaboration, and its impending product.

In corridors, we do this when we briefly coordinate plans to work on projects together or when we set up lunch with one another with the goal of establishing rapport, trust, and an alliance.

During meetings, we do this when we give each other our undivided attention, and we give affirming eye contact. As we listen intently to each other's talking-points, we publically note how a specific idea resonated with us and why. This is how we acknowledge and encourage each other to impart insight that otherwise would not be noted. A character like Ms. Uneasy would appreciate having this understanding within the space *she* occupies, because she felt irrelevant and alone.

We must make our connections honest and true as a covenant for other Black, professional, educated women to witness and to ritualize, because when one succeeds, we all succeed. When one fails, we all fail.

PART 2

"White Spaces" in High Places

CHAPTER 4

Be Aware of Gray Shade

Sharing the spotlight does not make one's light less bright

Mrs. Gray completed her requirements as a doctoral candidate and is now Dr. Gray. She is tall; she is brown, she wears her hair natural, and she is among five others who lead in a large organization that services over 12,000 stakeholders. She is an orator, because she is well-spoken;

she is prepared, and she is automatic, but thoughtful in her responses. Upon first glance, she makes the Black, professional, educated woman proud. She appears to be the example of the reality and not the cliché of our existence.

Her profile is an elite representation, and her contribution is a part within the whole; this positioning is what draws light to the unexposed truth. Her spotlight shines and reveals a powerful message to onlookers – that grace and class sit at the bowels of our wombs; wombs that create more of the same – from mother to daughter and so on.

Unfortunately, Dr. Gray believes she owns the patent, and she believes that she is the only one that can possess it. Her goal seems to be to ensure that there can only be one-at-a-time, and that one is she.

<u>(#)</u>

During an episode of Jerry Seinfeld's *Netflix* special *Comedians in Cars Getting Coffee,* Seinfeld's guest Eddie Murphy, shares with him the reality of what I will call the *one-at-a-time* ideology. Murphy reflectively discusses how he came to know Richard Pryor – the edgy, hilarious, Black, male comedian – a pioneer in the game of comedy. At the time, Murphy, the new, edgy, hilarious, Black, male comedian had begun to blaze a trail of his own.

However, Murphy expresses that unbeknownst to him, nights when Pryor was supposed to perform or be in attendance at a given comedy spots, Pryor would pull up to the place and ask who was in attendance. Murphy recounts that any time the response included "Eddie Murphy," Pryor would allegedly excuse himself and leave.

As Murphy recollects the moment he first learned of Pryor's alleged antics, there was a disappointed somberness that seemed to engulf him regarding his idol. One would wonder if this was a sense of regret contributed to the unaddressed awkwardness, intimidation, and insecurity that resonated within Richard Pryor.

(#)

Moreover, after more than 14 years of a supermodel feud between Naomi Campbell and Tyra Banks, Banks invited Campbell on her self-titled talk show, *Tyra*, to recount and address what Banks explains as unfair and cruel bullying antics by Campbell. The two discussed the nature of the industry, and the fact that Tyra's position as the new beautiful Black supermodel was a threat to Campbell, because of the *one-at-a-time* ideology that challenged Campbell's role within the modeling industry. The two also discussed how the industry perpetuated this notion, and only worsened the rivalry.

Like Pryor and Campbell, Dr. Gray did not become emboldened by the pressures associated with the system of this condition, but instead folded under it, and only perpetuated the *one-at-a-time* ideology. Although Dr. Gray had a seat at the table, she did not possess the character to contribute to it. When other Black professional educated women had been discredited or undervalued for work that far exceeded expectations, she was not compelled to be their voice at the table. Instead, she opted to believe that there is only room for one – *her*.

(#)

There is this notion that the "white space" does not encourage multiple Black people to fill the same arena, whether that space is a company or an industry. This vignette depicts this reality through Dr. Gray's story; she is also Mrs. Arrogant and the former Mrs. Gray in the previous chapters.

As a result of this unspoken rule that is understood and perpetuated by individual's like Dr. Gray, many overly qualified Black, professional, educated women get stiff-armed out of opportunities or dismissed from organizations when their ability seems to unintentionally undermine those of her constituents.

A Word of Advice

Recognize the value of another Black woman, so she can recognize it in you, and you will empower one another through your mutual acknowledgement.

Dr. Gray is gifted with a regality that she holds hostage. Oftentimes when a capable mentor, such as Dr. Gray, decides to mentor, she finds a mentee on the outside. The outside could mean a woman that is not Black or a Black woman that is not a part of the same network.

Maybe it is fear that one's successor might surpass them. Matthew 10:24 says, "The student is not above the teacher, nor a servant above his master," which in spirit, discredits such fear altogether. Furthermore, every prodigy needs a capable forerunner to refine them with the purpose to maintain the forward progress, such scaffolding should be tradition.

David Viscott's quote, "The meaning of life is to find your gift. The purpose of life is to give your gift away" is especially relevant, because Dr. Gray should have identified

other Black, professional, educated women from within her

arena to guide and to gift.

CHAPTER 5

Mr. Chip A. Waye

A first encounter with Napoleon

He despises her – not for her excellence alone, but for being an excellent woman with *that* skin. Ms. Kara Mell catches Mr. Chip A. Waye in the midst of his fixed gaze upon her left profile, and when she does, he is forced to snap out of his moment. It is as if someone placed a wake-up potion underneath his nostrils. He blinks and then vaguely shakes his head to get out of his thought.

In a fraction of a second, Kara decides that she has caught this gaze before, but this is the first time she has ever received it from a man – more specifically, a white one. She suspects it is time to bring her brief report to a close.

Kara begins to listen to her other colleagues' reports, and she observes Chip's eye-contact with them. She does not see the same look of what she assessed a moment ago to be a sneer in his eyes. Kara is an effective Project Manager that the company's CEO recently transferred to this up-and-coming department, which Chip oversees as Director.

The meeting is adjourned. As Kara collects her laptop and ID from the conference room table, and as she begins to head back to her office, she says to herself, "I wonder what that was about." She *almost* makes this a concern. However, Kara chalks it up to the fact that she is new to the team, and he is probably just processing what she had said during her report. At the next meeting, Kara again catches Chip in this fixed gaze. Although Kara is a very attractive woman, she understands that his gaze does not communicate attraction, and she gets a suspicion that he has covered up his unattraction for women by marrying one.

Over time, she begins reading into subtle nuances from him. During these meetings, Kara is always about business; however, just before the Project Managers' meeting with Chip, he catches Kara in a moment of exchanged niceties and laughter with a colleague. With a tone of condescension, Chip says to Kara, but he does not say to the other colleague, "*You* look happy today." Feeling the insult of his passive aggressiveness, she thinks, "His feedback is absent when it has to do with the projects I'm managing, but my *looks* receive feedback?" As the meeting proceeds, she is in her head for what feels like an eternity, but is more like 30 seconds.

She recalls her first introduction with Chip about seven weeks back. It was within the common area of his office; she and Chip greeted one another for the first time. "Hello, Mr. Waye," she said to him with a smile and extended hand, "It is a pleasure meeting you. I look forward to working with you and learning of what my assignments will be." Chip looked up to Kara, because he stands at about 5 feet 5 inches tall, and he shook her hand in return. He said, "Yes. Um. I look forward to having you here. I don't know much *about* you, but I *don't* listen to the commentary of others." Upon hearing this, Kara believed her face wasn't easily readable, but was not sure if her truth had emanated from a wrinkle over the corner of her mouth; she thought, "*Wow*, that is a snarky thing to say to someone you're just meeting for the first time."

In that moment, she remembers her *previous* department. She had been alienated by her team – two females, one Project Manager and the other – their

Director. The two would host informal meetings with one another and make plans without including Kara in the process, and when Kara was present, they would often speak in Spanish, and then revert to English to appear as if they were including her.

Nonetheless, Kara felt their inconvenience all the same; to note the unprofessionalism of their behavior would most definitely be perceived as unjust from their stance. However, Kara dealt with their false English-speaking accommodation for two years working within that area of the organization. It was particularly difficult for her – especially since most of the stakeholders were Spanish-speaking. Therefore, when the CEO presented the opportunity to work with Chip, Kara looked at it as one.

Kara snaps back to the present moment, and it dawns on her; she begins to feel the epiphany move through her bloodstream like a cool breeze, "*That* is why Chip's gaze was so familiar to me; I caught my previous Director in one of those moments."

Kara wonders if this discernment is God's way of preparing her for more of these intentional acts of alienation to come.

A Word of Advice

When Kara left her first Director behind, she did so without having closure, and she did so without having a strategy for addressing it should it happen again in another context. If she had given it more thought, she might have anticipated some of the methods used to alienate her at her next venture, and she might have had a more automatic response to it when it surfaced.

For instance, when Chip first formally met Kara, and said, "Yes. Um. I look forward to having you here. I don't know much *about* you, but I *don't* listen to the commentary of others." Kara could have done more than make a mental note of Chip's "snarky" comment when it happened, since the first impression is the most important.

Chip's "snarky" comment was purposeful; he said it with an intention to disempower her. Therefore, she could have simply challenged him to explain himself. Kara might have said with a matter-or-fact tone, "Oh, please don't stop there. Enlighten me. What commentary and from whom?"

Having been challenged and most likely not expecting it,

Chip would either retract his statement or downplay it.

Nonetheless, Kara would have put Chip on notice.

The notice: "Be careful; I know what game you're

playing, but if you want to keep playing, I win."

CHAPTER 6

Who are "They"

"They" collude in a vacuum

*T*hey are the *darkness* in every institution. "They" generally fall within two categories and are extremely aware of the category in which "They" belong: 1) ineffectual and political or 2) intelligent and lazy. "They" find one another. Thereby, creating an entourage of psychological and intellectual chaos for *those* on the other side of their scheme.

"Those" who fall on the other side are the *Light* in every institution, and comprise two categories: 1) effective and nonpolitical or 2) intelligent and ambitious.

It is immediately that "They" recognize "Those", who are their direct opposite, and despise them for it, because "They" perceive them as a threat to their existence in any organizational bureaucracy. Pulling from their strengths, "They" use their politics and intelligence to undermine *those* "They" deem as a threat.

To align themselves with one another, "They" say contemptuous things about their victim. For instance, "They" might plant a seed by saying something like, "Kara *seems* to think of herself quite *highly* now that she is in her *new* department; those under her may *actually* like her, because she has *presence*." The tester would wait to see how the tested responds. If the tested responds sincerely with something like, "She *does* have great presence, and I have heard that she's *really* quite capable," then it's a fail; no new recruit, but if the tested responds pompously with something like, "Yeah. I noticed that she *thinks* of herself quite highly; the way she walks around here, *humph!* But, I *guess* she *does* have – What did you say? – *Presence*." "They" have found themselves a new recruit.

"They" have strength within institutions, because of their savviness with the game of politics, so when "Those" whose ability naturally outshines them are on display, "They" see it as a threat to their political positioning. "They" fear "Those" with the ability to eclipse them, because "They" fear the loss of political power "They" have gained through connecting with other marginal constituents and through aligning themselves with authority figureheads within the organization by planting seeds of treachery.

So, "They" are plotting, while "Those" with ability are producing.

A Word of Advice

"Those" who are producing must continue to do so, but also be equipped to outmaneuver the plots of their opposition. "They" have positioned themselves politically within the organization, and "They" have done so through personalizing working relationships, and gaining close proximity to the ear and to the trust of those with authority.

"They" make themselves reliable to those with authority – not by doing what is in the best interest of the organization with excellence, but by using their charisma to gain favor.

Oftentimes, the one with authority is not *just* concerned with excellence; authority figures like to laugh too; they like their ego stroked just as much as the next one, and "They" have studied the authority well enough to know how to gain their favor, but beware, "They" have also studied you.

Whereas, "Those" who produce stay fixated on producing for the sake of the good; it is natural for them to do this. It is their only focus, which leads to their demise in any organizational bureaucracy, because "They" inflict guerrilla warfare tactics, and "Those" on the other side of it are not prepared to deal with it, because of their bureaucratic naivety.

Therefore, it is the job of the "Those" who are the light and the merit of the organization to be aware of how "They" are playing the game, in order to be steps ahead of any manipulation or political maneuvers "They" make.

Such is the game created and led by the "white space".

CHAPTER 7
Chip

When someone tells you who they are, believe them

Kara begins to snap out of the moment she spent in her head, and she finds her short gaze has been fixed upon her notepad – her pen is in the act of a circular motion that creates an almost microscopic doddle. Could this circular trance be symbolic of the full circle she's experienced with passive aggressive workplace alienation? The residual effects of her dreamy state had not completely subsided, but she decides that Chip's snide comments, his lack of constructive feedback, and his unpleasant gaze do not change how she views her commitment to the projects she oversees.

A couple of months go by, and due to her weekly meetings with her team of employees, Kara is feeling positive and productive, because her team is gelling beautifully, and she has managed to make small gains with them that she is confident will soon translate into long-term growth and sustainability.

The Project Ball is the company's annual professional development workshop that Project Managers host with their respective teams, and it is fast approaching. This is the opportunity for Directors to visit and evaluate the Project Managers who report to them. Kara is excited about this chance to receive real constructive feedback, because she often wonders if the weekly Project Manager's meetings with

Chip are even sufficient enough for him to get a true sense of how she's managing her projects and team.

She cannot help but think that her 1 minute report is often saturated by his secret gaze. It's a solid 15-seconds of blankness that he inserts somewhere in her briefing. She thinks to herself, "Great! Chip will now be able to see and experience the work that I've been doing."

At this point, Kara has already convinced herself to believe that Chip has been giving her space. She tells herself that for a valid reason he has not attended any of her meetings or checked in on her at all – unless she counts the day they met in his office several months ago. She chalks it up to the notion that he is letting her acclimate herself with the department, with *the* team, and with *her* team.

She is beginning to *honor* Chip for her distorted perception of his leadership approach, and is thrilled that Chip will be visiting her workshop – especially since she is the new Project Manager in his department. Kara has prepared her team for this workshop; one she calls *Building the Next Leaders.*

The event begins with a powerfully inspiring presentation in the auditorium, and then everyone is dispersed to their respective conference rooms. Feeling empowered, Kara cruises upon the adrenaline, and so her energy flows smoothly into her workshop. Her team like any other day displays invigoration and engagement.

It is getting to the middle of Kara's workshop, and Chip has yet to visit, but she is still hopeful that Chip will make his way to her conference room. She thinks, "This is a great time for him to come in. The team is presenting charts and graphs. I am asking poignant questions for the group to grapple, reconsider, rehash, and reconstruct."

Kara has a clear view of the hallway. She spots Chip leaving one of the other Project Manager's workshop, and she sees that he is steadily approaching her conference room. A flutter of positive anxiety fills her soul with each nearing step. She believes Chip will be pleased with his newest Project Manager and the work she is doing for him and his department – to build competent and excited future leaders.

Chip is only a few paces from entering Kara's conference room, and the two lock eyes. Kara smiles, and Chip *rapidly* turns away – as if he hoped that Kara had not noticed, he swiftly passes her conference room. "What just happened?" Kara briefly puzzles through the pieces to unlock an acceptable scenario. "He'll be back. He must have to handle something really important," she convinces herself.

She shakes the feeling of disappointment, and she transitions to the last part of the workshop, so she has her team break out into smaller groups. As bodies are shuffling around the space, Kara spots Chip heading back into the conference room he had left 5 minutes earlier. Kara believes that Chip will shortly make his way to her workshop. Her anxiety morphs to hope – hope that Chip will make time to see the work she has been doing with her team in the last four months.

Kara is having a private battle that only she knows exists. 30-minutes later she transitions to the closing of the first Project Ball she has ever done with this department. 5-minutes later the hallways begin to fill with staff – a sign that the Project Ball is now officially over. "Maybe, he only had time to visit the one workshop," Kara justifies, but the absurdity of the justification sets in when she thinks, "It was a 4-hour event, and he only has *four* Project Managers."

At the next weekly Project Managers' meeting with Chip, through informal dialogue before the meeting officially starts, Kara learns from the other Project Managers that Chip had visited their respective workshops. Two of them for an hour and a half, and one for an hour. In that moment of realization, Kara feels rejected.

Knowing Chip is hearing this chit chat, and wanting to get a look of remorse or inexperience from Chip's face for having left her out, Kara looks over at him; he does not

expect Kara to move so quickly from realization, to rejection,

and then to him, so Kara catches Chip already looking at her,

and she can see a glimpse of satisfaction living at the corners

of his mouth. He had been secretly savoring Kara's

revelation that she does not belong. His look said, "As long

as I can help it, she never will."

Caught, Chip goes with it; he embraces it, and he says

with the intent of malice, but with an even tone; one that only

Kara can fully perceive, "Kara, that's why you and the team

do your weekly reports. Though yours only lasts about a

minute, I have enough to know how you're doing. Ok?" His

"ok" was more of an expression of finality, and not an

expression of inquiry.

Though blistering within her is this truth that she is

being treated differently than the other Project Managers,

who are either white or white-Latina, Kara does not want to

accept it. Still, she decides that she will not allow herself to be a victim, and she chalks it up to circumstance and moves on – like she did last time in her previous department.

After the winter holidays, Kara wants to discuss a new project with Chip for his approval, so she attempts to set up a meeting with him. Excited about the nature of the project, Kara requests a morning meeting for the following week. The next day Kara notices an email from Chip to her that was sent the night before. It is an email that reads, "Meeting Request Rejected," so Kara requests another early meeting, and that is rejected as well.

Not wanting to believe this is intentional, at the next Project Managers' meeting with Chip, she brings it to his attention. He encourages Kara to make another request. He says, "Ok. Just send me another invite." Even still, request-after-request, Chip rejects them all.

Kara Mell officially decides that Chip A. Waye is not interested in scaffolding her progress as her Director nor does he want to evaluate her in truth, so he uses passive aggressive methods in his attempt to deflate her in the most passable way possible. He is not interested in Kara's leadership abilities, since he is most interested in chipping away at it.

(#)

Over the years, my Dad and I have had very in-depth conversations about various interpersonal connections, which constitutes family, friend, and organizational relationships. I would share with him a particularly unpleasant exchange I had – a buildup scenario much like Kara's, and looking for advice without directly asking him, he would know it and say, "When someone tells you who they are, believe them."

Unfortunately for Kara, she took too long to process it, because she ended up feeling disappointed and rejected as a result. Kara's previous Director and the other Project Manager, both were territorial women, and Kara's current Director is an insecure man. Chip has certainly shown Kara who he is, but it was up to Kara to believe it instead of making excuses for him.

Since Chip and Kara's previous team are all very threatened by the value of an attractive, knowledgeable, Black women with promise and presence, they found the only way they could attempt to extinguish the threat – to alienate it.

A Word of Advice

To minimize the threat of upstaging your insecure superior, learn the game of politics "they" play so well, so you might want to identify positive feedback you can sparingly and authentically give your threatened boss when he or she is among other constituents, but make sure the positive feedback also sheds a modest light on what makes you valuable to the organization.

For instance, "I am lucky to have a Director like Chip, because I can be quite creative since he truly honors invigorating ideas – like, I'm doing a *Building Future Leaders* presentation for the Project Ball, and I will be using all of these new technologies that are best practices in our field. And thanks to Chip, me and my team is really looking forward to what we have been building upon; it should be exciting." So, instead of Kara just giving a generic report that did not include Chip, she could have infused Chip into her report by giving him kudos for supporting her efforts. The likelihood of Chip feeling threatened would have been low, and the likelihood of him attending her workshop would have been high.

If the threat remains, do not give it too much more of your emotional attention. Continue to be excellent, but continue to be aware of political moves *you* need to make to maintain your position if you would like to continue to be a part of the organization. Remember, "they" will likely make their political moves to your disadvantage.

Also, start pouring into your gift outside of work, because you might be creating an opportunity for yourself that translates into something you would not have otherwise imagined – like entrepreneurship.

Alienation is a tactic that is overplayed in the "white space", because its purpose is to subdue your effect within the organization, so that what "they" say about you, which is never good, seems true.

CHAPTER 8

In the Closet

"They" feel good when "they" enforce their power on you

Dr. Destiny Imani, a Nurse Practitioner, is kicking herself as she is making her way across town to the other office. She sits at a light – 10 minutes away, and the meeting with the Board of Directors starts *now*. In spite of the fall weather, she takes off her coat, and she turns the air conditioner up, because her nerves have already begun to transfer into pockets of bursting heat underneath her armpits, hands, and feet.

She says to herself, "It doesn't even matter that the meeting invitation was just noted on my calendar the night before, and that I noticed it this morning; it also doesn't matter that I took in an emergency patient, which is why I am running 10 minutes behind. I am *late*, and the Director that set up this meeting is not going to be empathetic." This thought sends a strong palpitation through her chest cavity, and she proceeds across town.

Destiny parks, grabs her bags, jumps out of the car, and then begins to regulate her heart beat as she makes her way into the building and takes the journey to the third floor. Destiny enters the conference room, and notices the only vacant chair is the one situated directly beside Mrs. Ivory. As cool as a cucumber, and as she finds her way to the vacant chair, Destiny quietly walks around the table, and exchanges a warm smile with her colleagues who are situated at the conference table. Before sitting, she places her coat at the back of this imposing chair, and she then gets into the seat.

As Destiny is situating herself in the chair, she is noticing the quiet in the room. There is a soft glow emanating from the LCD projector, and there is a graph projecting on the screen, but in this moment, Destiny says to herself, "It's quiet, and no one is saying a word." It is a fleeting thought. One that does not seem relevant, because Destiny considers, "Just *maybe* the meeting hasn't started yet – maybe other participants have just entered, and Mrs. Ivory is gracious to give everyone time to arrive."

Destiny makes eye contact with one of the nurses across from her at the table and imparts a smile and a whispered "Good afternoon." The nurse softly participates in the cordial exchange. Mrs. Ivory says to Destiny for the group to hear, "*Now* that you have arrived, Dr. Imani, we can start." Destiny responds with astonishment, "Wow. You waited for *me*?" Destiny thinks to herself, "This isn't my meeting; *I* – *I* know I'm late, but was it necessary to wait for *me*?"

Mrs. Ivory continues, "Unfortunately, since we waited for you to arrive, we are going to be 15 minutes behind schedule, and I am also going to have to push back all of my other meetings, which means *they* will be waiting." Destiny feels the attempt to embarrass her more than the embarrassment itself, and she also notices the subtle discomfort and lack of eye-contact by the rest of the meeting's participants; Destiny says with a smile to Mrs. Ivory, "Let's talk later."

Mrs. Ivory starts the meeting, and Destiny moves on, and like her colleagues at the table, Destiny wholeheartedly imparts into the flow of the meeting. However, Mrs. Ivory is looking to rehash; she cannot *stand* the idea that this young, Black, woman is a Nurse Practitioner for one of the top-rated hospitals on the East Coast; Mrs. Ivory's skin crawls knowing that this young, Black, woman who is 12 years younger, but whom she supposes is 17 years younger, has advanced her education to the highest level. Written upon Mrs. Ivory's face is the thought virus that spread there. If expressions could talk, Mrs. Ivory's faces says, "*She*, Dr. Imani, has the *audacity* to show up to *my* meeting late."

Mrs. Ivory cannot suppress her even deeper-seeded thought: "Who does this nigger think *she* is, coming to *my* meeting late?" As if seething with hot boiling oil on the inside, Mrs. Ivory is out for revenge, and so she seizes an opportunity to cultivate her inner most thoughts in a way that can be successful in this environment.

Destiny does not – at first notice, but as she imparts input along with her colleagues, Mrs. Ivory blankly stares and then blatantly redirects to find input elsewhere. It is not until Destiny realizes an unspoken wince that befalls her colleagues that she then perceives Mrs. Ivory's subtle act as an added attempt to embarrass her among colleagues.

86

Nonetheless, Destiny decides that she will brush off Mrs. Ivory's antics for now, and she maintains an even disposition throughout the meeting. However, Destiny can't help but suppose that Mrs. Ivory's antics toward her is expressing something more deep-seeded than Destiny's tardiness to this meeting.

The meeting is adjourned, and colleagues exchange niceties as they each pick up their personal belongings – a delay that prevents them from heading out of the meeting right away. Destiny collects her things slowly. She is observing Mrs. Ivory, because she cannot fathom that Mrs. Ivory had forgotten her suggestion to, "talk later." Destiny is also modelling discretion since Mrs. Ivory forfeited such respect earlier. Destiny notices Mrs. Ivory trying to make an escape – in her attempt to maneuver around someone standing just before the threshold of the door. Mrs. Ivory's try at sliding out of the ashes unscathed is unsuccessful.

Destiny asserts, "Mrs. Ivory. Do you mind if we meet briefly before you head out?" Mrs. Ivory's bones rattle underneath her skin, and a few of their colleagues take a subtle peak over their shoulders, while trying to maintain their respective conversations on their way out of the conference room. "Oh! Sure, Dr. Imani. Let me find a place since my office is likely occupied." Destiny walks into the corridor with her belongings and awaits confirmation that a room is available for this brief meeting. Mrs. Ivory returns, "Ok, Dr. Imani. Come with me."

Dr. Imani follows Mrs. Ivory to an office where two receptionists are seated at separate desks. She enters a door within the original space; she turns on the light, and then takes Destiny through the door. Destiny almost does not realize the absurdity of the scenario, because in her mind she is choosing her words concisely.

Mrs. Ivory says, "Dr. Imani, how can I help you?" Destiny's gesture is a metaphoric visual of putting a thing to the side while she says, "Before I start, I would like to ask that we first put our titles to the side." Destiny continues, "I want to first apologize for my tardiness. There is no excuse for that. However, person-to-person I would have appreciated a private reprimand as opposed to a public one."

Mrs. Ivory defends, "I believe a public notation was necessary, because it impacted everyone." Destiny realizes that this is something that Mrs. Ivory will have to work out on her own, but Destiny believes she clearly expressed in a professional way the importance of her humanity to one that attempted to violate it. Destiny was not looking for agreeance.

Destiny begins to head back down to the parking lot, so she can return to the other office. She runs over some of the events to self-reflect and then self-evaluate. She opens the door of her car, and she sits for some time allowing the events to appropriately process before deciding to press the button to start the ignition, which would essentially be her pressing the snap-out-of-it button and choosing to move on with the rest of her day. And then, it dawns on her that the one-on-one meeting that she and Mrs. Ivory just had – was in a closet.

(#)

No one is perfect, and though many Black, professional, educated women cannot get the light shined on her for the things she does well, the light will surely shine on her when she makes a mistake no matter how small or insignificant. The shine will attempt to penetrate the core of her Black womanhood by casting a piercing light upon her with the hope of discovering or exhuming her blemishes.

Though Destiny makes a mistake, it does not speak for the essence of her excellence, and though she makes a mistake, the attempt to diminish her value is amiss, because she maintains her posture. When a Black woman owns her character, it becomes the envy of onlookers who see her blackness and her womanhood as a threat. Too frequently attempts at intimidating and bullying her allows her to show onlookers how she rises from such antics with such grace and class, and it concurrently takes her on a quest toward her self-awareness packed with strength, power, and endurance.

However, Destiny does not realize the depths that Mrs. Ivory would go to try to belittle her. Mrs. Ivory's antics, to take Destiny into a closet, speaks to how Mrs. Ivory sees herself in relation to how she sees Destiny, and Mrs. Ivory does not flinch to perform degrading acts against her. However, Destiny sees Mrs. Ivory for who *she* really is – a woman that takes advantage of the "white space", because she is one of its beneficiaries. *That* is Mrs. Ivory's posture.

A Word of Advice

When someone challenges your character, maintain your posture. The way you do this is with constant self-talk. The moment your ego attempts to pull you toward instant gratification – like sending a combative email or addressing the offender angrily, you will have lost. If you succumb to your emotions, you should know that it will only play into the hands of your challenger. Instead, tell yourself that you will continue to behave in a way that is above the fray.

If you have been publically ridiculed, make a *public* note that you will address your concern in private. Destiny does this when she first publically states to Mrs. Ivory, "Let's talk later," and then she publically follows through when she says, "Mrs. Ivory. Do you mind if we meet briefly before you head out?" Destiny maintains her posture, because she stays professional, unemotional, and as a result, above the fray; she publically notes she will address Mrs. Ivory, and in spite of the location and regardless of Mrs. Ivory's stance, Destiny

executes in the private moment.

CHAPTER 9

Bandits Exist in the Green Space

Ms. Nia's Achilles heel

"Ms. Nia! Get to the main office, *now*! And bring your laptop!" Vice Principal, Mrs. Negrita's voice is a penetrating blare over the walkie-talk. Ms. Nia is a high school Vice Principal, and the appointed School Testing Coordinator, who is in the middle of wrapping up 9th grade PSAT testing. Ms. Nia is confused, and thinks to herself, "Why is my friend – my colleague, Mrs. Negrita on the walkie-talkie making this piercing demand?" Ms. Nia's nerves rattle inside of her, and she grabs her walkie-talkie, grabs her laptop, grabs her all-access ID badge, and grabs her laptop charger, and then she makes her way to the front of the building.

On her way, through long corridors, she collects her rattling nerves in an effort to reserve them for the unknown she is about to walk into, and just as she gets into the main office, she passes the main conference room, and she notices three figures huddling together, wearing invisible white coned hoods that the naked eye just cannot see, but Ms. Nia's intuition is throbbing on high alert; it is an instinctual warning message to her that there is degrading activity in close proximity. The three figures in the middle of conjuring a scheme are Mrs. Haman, Ms. Delilah, and Mr. Cain.

Mrs. Haman is an Assistant Superintendent, Ms. Delilah is a Supervisor, and Mr. Cain is Ms. Nia's direct supervisor, the Principal. As she passes the conference room, it is in this split instant that Ms. Nia processes what she is witnessing, and she consequently takes two steps back to position herself at the entrance of the conference room; she feels in the marrow of her bones that Mrs. Negrita's alert and these three figures conspiring *must* be related, so to show the conspirators that she *sees* them, Ms. Nia remains standing at the threshold of the door and feigns a salutation; the purpose of this action serves more as an acknowledgement of her witness account to their antics.

Mrs. Haman is caught off guard and says, "Oh, hey Ms. Nia! How'd testing go?" Ms. Nia responds, "It went well. I was just wrapping things up." Mrs. Haman says as fake as faux, "Oh, that's good," and the two others stand as if someone had just pressed pause, and they had been immovable – only blinking and breathing.

Ms. Nia excuses herself, and she enters Mr. Cain's office where the rest of her Vice Principal colleagues had been sitting: Mrs. Negrita, a black-Latina, who is known to prioritize students by any means necessary; Ms. Blanco, a white-Latina, who is known to be wicked to all of the stakeholders: teachers, students, and security officers, and Mr. Waddams, a white man, who stays under the radar in his decision-making, while concurrently having a "yes man" nature that is obviously tied to his job security.

There was a strange silence that had befallen the atmosphere of this space, so to break up the monotony of it all, Ms. Nia gets up and plugs her laptop charger into the wall, and then she sits to the left of Mrs. Negrita. No one makes eye-contact. It is a weirdness sweating from the walls and dripping from Ms. Nia's colleagues, but no one is bold enough to say what it is, and Ms. Nia is not sure if she wants to ask Mrs. Negrita in the presence of her other colleagues.

To her, it seems as if a conversation to which she had not been privy had just taken place. Now in the presence of the one foaming at the mouth on the walkie talkie, Mrs. Negrita says nothing. So, Ms. Nia figures that she has no reason to worry, but she also senses that whatever this meeting is about *must* be quite urgent, so along with her colleagues, she waits.

(#)

Mr. Cain's previous experience as an educator and as an administrator had been limited. As a teacher, he taught Music, and as an administrator, he served as a junior high school Vice Principal for one-year, and at that time, he served under a tyrant of a principal, who happened to have great affection for him. When the high school principal position opened, the tyrant was said to have it, but the tyrant enjoyed the comfort and feasibility of his longtime position, and therefore recommended his Vice Principal, Mr. Cain, who egotistically and naively dove head first into the opportunity.

Going into Mr. Cain's third year as high school Principal, he had already accrued major and consistent cracks in his leadership, and so the senior administration had him as a specimen sitting under lenses magnified 1000 times. When the Superintendent of Schools placed Ms. Nia on Mr. Cain's leadership team as one of his four Vice Principals, he overanalyzed it, and at the beginning, he treaded lightly around her.

His only reference to Ms. Nia was the quarterly district administrators' meetups, and the monthly administrative meetings. He heard her speak in participation at these forums, and he noticed the Superintendent and other senior administrators accept her input with great consideration and affirmation.

What was actually respect for her competence, Mr. Cain perceived as favoritism and cronyism. Therefore, he thought that the Superintendent had placed Ms. Nia on his team as either of two things: 1) a spy or 2) a replacement.

As a strategy to stay good with the senior administration, Mr. Cain would tell Ms. Nia that he shared his approval of her participation on his team with the senior administrators, and Ms. Nia could sense his false and condescendingly limited acknowledgement of her work and input. As a result, she would experience this rumbling feeling inside her, because his purview of the work she had been doing up to this point was intentionally distant. However, she was confident that overtime his insincerity would come to find truth in how she handles her assignments.

Unfortunately for Ms. Nia, Mr. Cain had already pegged her as threat, and nothing – not even learning that Ms. Nia had no real connection to the Superintendent of Schools and not even learning that Ms. Nia had not been placed as a spy or a replacement would change the callous he grew because of his misconception of her placement, and his disdain for her competence. Instead, it only gave him permission to conspire a conservative attack on Ms. Nia's reputation.

Mr. Cain's deep-seeded vengeance for Ms. Nia is rooted in something almost Shakespearean. His arrogance is embedded in the story he manufactured of the emotional and verbal abuse he experienced because of his father. His mother, a first-hand witness to the scope of the relationship between father and son never perceived her son as abused – physically, emotionally or sexually – not because she was in denial or inattentive, but because it simply did not exist.

When Mr. Cain was a child, he was his mother's shadow; he clung to her like some nasty lice to clean hair. His mother and father were polar opposites; this Betty Crocker meets Ralph Kramden scenario. His father would hold him accountable for his behavior, while his mother would gloss it over, and oftentimes, in the presence of their son, she would tell her husband that he was wrong to reprimand him. The two would rarely have conflict, but the only conflict Mr. Cain witnessed were based around his discipline.

Overtime, Mr. Cain was consumed by a festering notion that his mother was not truly happy with his father, and he allowed his conjuring to corrupt him. This was the start of a strangely lascivious plot to do damage. He wanted to get his father back for being the only one to ever hold him accountable for his spoiled behavior.

Even into adulthood, Mr. Cain openly discussed with half-strangers the half-truth of his mother and father's relationship. "I could sense her unhappiness," Ms. Nia remembers hearing him say to a couple of their team members at the end of small-talk. Yet another glitch in reality is the idea that he convinced himself that all of this "unhappiness" talk was true. Oddly, *he* believed that he would be the one to make her happy.

Just as his mother was not aware of the non-existent abuse of her son, she also was not aware of her lack of correction that contributed to his deficient maturation process from boyhood into manhood. She merely assumed she was raising a sensitive young man that would grow up to be a compassionate adult; however, her rearing had quite the opposite effect. Her lack of correction was equivalent to taking away his accountability in life, and it only created flaws in his character from the start. One flaw being a sense of entitlement, and as a result he also lacked empathy and capacity.

Mr. Cain privately enjoyed the woes of the downtrodden in spite of their efforts. He is the image of a sinisterly seething boy placing a magnify glass just above an ant that relentlessly does all it can to avoid the unavoidable laser-like sun rays; the ant's inevitable demise.

Though his father was madly in love with his mother, and she in love him, his father was also aware of the potential stain his wife's coddling would cause their son, and so he took on the role as disciplinarian, which created an unrepairable wedge in their marriage, and Mr. Cain secretly enjoyed the demise of his father's spirit. It was an ecstasy that planted a seed that only grew wilder as Mr. Cain grew older.

(#)

Unbeknownst to Ms. Nia, Ms. Delilah, the Supervisor, was promised Ms. Nia's position, but Ms. Nia was selected for it. The two even share the same departments and oversee many of the same teachers. Ms. Nia's Achilles heel was not knowing she had a rival so close to her. While Mrs. Haman, one of the Assistant Superintendents, is the new kid on the block with much to prove and many bullets in the trigger to pull, and so the three figures conspire in the conference room, while Ms. Nia awaits the inevitable.

Mr. Cain enters his office where Ms. Nia is checking emails regarding the day's testing, and as the three Vice

Principals sit in this strange silence, Mr. Cain taps Ms. Nia on the shoulder, and he leans in close to her left ear to say, "Ms. Nia, Mrs. Haman and I need you in the conference room."

(#)

There are many competent people in positions, because of *what* they know, and there are many competent people in positions – not just because they have the skill, but because of *who* they know. Similarly, there are many incompetent people in positions – without skill, but because of *who* they know.

In the case of Mr. Cain, he was incompetent and without skill for the job, but because of his confidence in his ability to manipulate the truth, he found success in aligning himself with people of authority, and with them, he manufactured a shared agenda. While Ms. Nia was competent in her position, her motivation was not to plot and scheme and to align herself with people of authority, but to

105

be effective in her role and to allow her work to speak for itself.

As a child, Mr. Cain developed this Oedipus complex, and a disdain for his father, which was the basis for his positioning for authority as a child. In adulthood, Ms. Nia's competence and perceived rapport with senior administration was a threat, which is why Mr. Cain initially spoke to senior administrators about his favor of Ms. Nia. He thought he could get in good with them through her.

However, when he realized she was not as connected as he thought, her ability remained a threat to his position.

A Word of Advice

This vignette is a testament to the true nature of the "white space". This is how it feels, and this is how it conspires – through politics, so trust your intuition and respond early.

Do not wait for a person that has the authority to replace you to build upon false knowledge of you – *especially* when it threatens your position. Ms. Nia had the feeling that things were not right between she and Mr. Cain, but she may have underestimated his position with the senior administrators – considering he was under their microscope.

Even still, when he told her that he spoke favorably of her, he gave her an indication that despite his incompetence, he did in fact have their ear and potentially their trust. In the same way, he claimed to have spoken favorably about her, he eventually spoke negatively about her to create a narrative that she was not privy to, and she was later replaced without being given the respect and the courtesy to tell her truth. All an indication that whatever picture he had painted of her, they believed. Therefore, the safest position is to be both competent and aligned with the ones pulling the strings.

It is also safe to say that Ms. Nia identifies as "Those" who are competent *but* unpolitical, while Mr. Cain identifies as "They" that are incompetent *but* political. Like so many of "Those" who are not concerned with bureaucratic politics, Ms. Nia loses a battle she does not even know she is in.

Her failing is the result of her inability to separate the notion of building a genuine rapport with senior administrators from simply being a brownnoser of them. Such a rapport might have created an opportunity for senior administrators to see her excellence on their own.

Through the rapport Mr. Cain built with Mrs. Haman, he certainly used cunning antics to eradicate the potential threat to his position as Principal, and though Ms. Nia did not want to play the game of politics, she needed to use the same strategies Mr. Cain used in order for her to maintain the position she worked so hard to achieve.

By necessity, Ms. Nia should have positioned herself in close proximity to those with the authority to eventually decide upon her tenure. She could have genuinely, but intentionally fostered a rapport through creating direct opportunities to be seen as reliable and communicative. This way, authority figures could have formulated their own assessment of Ms. Nia's character and work ethic instead of relying upon direct reports from her supervisor, Mr. Cain. Whatever their decision, she could have been content knowing that she had a handle on her own fate. Surely, by doing so, she may still have her job.

"Those" who are like Ms. Nia have integrity, because of their skill, their drive, their intellect, and their right intentions, but like Ms. Strategist from one of the earlier vignettes – know the game well enough to be ahead of the players that are out to win by any means necessary, because one's professional experience depends on it.

Rapport building is the best tactic for "Those" within organizations, who are competent *but* unpolitical, because at the end of the day, and behind closed doors, "They" will attempt to undermine their opposition. However, genuine rapport and true capacity will have the final say.

PART 3

Filling in the "White Spaces"

A word of advice

CHAPTER 10

Avoiding a Void

A "white space" in Branding

*D*ove started what is known as the *Campaign for Real Beauty* in the early 2000s. Katherine Froehlich's article, "Dove: Changing the Face of Beauty" notes regarding the company. Olivia Johnson's article, "How Dove Changed the Rules of the Beauty Game" discusses how *Unilever* originally launched *Dove* as a soap brand in 1951, and 50 years later in 2001, the company had "fundamentally changed," and with that change came a need for a new advertising campaign. To figure out how to set their brand apart from the heavily populated personal care market, *Dove* assembled a branding team composed mostly of women.

The team examined the brand and decided to make beauty its focus. Johnson notes, "Each member had the intuitive sense that the way other beauty brands behaved was not quite right (in the moral sense, not the commercial sense)." So, what was wrong? Johnson notes, "It was the type of beauty promoted by these brands – it was all about a physical idea that most [people – especially women] fall short of. This made the members of the global team feel miserable about themselves."

Froehlich reports that, "As a result, the team got to work and ultimately turned their dismay about the beauty market into the *Campaign for Real Beauty*. Advertisements [were] launched around the world asking if they had shown women (none of whom fit the 'global standard') [who] were 'wrinkled or wonderful,' 'oversized or outstanding,' and 'gray or gorgeous.'"

Dove made a business decision to include the voices of women to identify a "white space" that existed within the world of beauty. What they had discovered might not have ever been addressed if the differing perspectives of older women and plus-sized women were not included at the table. That is why having a *seat* at the table, especially as it pertains to decision-making that impacts groups of people with similar experiences, is paramount. Having their perspectives noted at the table, made way for a broader message to be expressed and universally understood.

On the other hand, Olivia Zed's article, "How Dove's Real Beauty campaign won, and nearly lost, its audience," states, "The campaign's impact extended beyond promoting a vision for beauty equality. Sales for *Dove* jumped from $2.5 to $4 billion in the campaign's first ten years. *Dove* bars became the number one preferred soap brand in the U.S. and *Unilever's* bestselling product company-wide."

However, at the same token, though women were included at the table, it seems that the voice of Black women was not present or simply was not heard or was silenced at the table, because Zed also notes, "In October 2017, *Dove* released a three-second body wash ad on Facebook. The ad featured a diverse trio of women individually lifting their shirts to transition into one another – a Black woman pulled up her shirt to reveal a white woman, who then unveiled an Asian woman."

Zed continues, "Depicting a Black woman transforming to white through soap was an unwitting nod to an ugly theme of 19th century advertising when blatantly racist messages suggested 'dirty' people of color could be purified to white with soap." Zed states, "Unsurprisingly, the ad swiftly incited a wave of criticism across social media denouncing *Dove* for racism. Global headlines in top-tier traditional media outlets followed."

Avoiding a void would mean to include representation of those missing, because to not have cultural representation or to culturally misrepresent people could be prevented with their welcomed input.

.

A Word of Advice

It is our societal and moral obligation to be conscious of voids and avoid them at all costs. If by human error, we are blindsided by an angle that no one has considered, and if proper representation is present when decisions are being made, we could rest assured that the void might be attributed to human error and not racial degradation. However, we still have a responsibility, because when the *Dove* commercial depicted a Black woman transitioning into a white woman after using a *Dove* soap bar, that should not have been the insult.

Instead, the insult should have been the reaction of those, who *only* saw something wrong with a Black woman transitioning into a white woman when other transitions had been made. This reaction digs into the depths of people's perceptions of Black women in relation to white women. Black is somehow dirty; it is somehow wrong, and it is somehow scary. In this context, and all other contexts:

117

business, socioeconomics, politics, media, and beauty, the "white space" subliminally positions itself as superior to Blackness. And, it reacts with propaganda as if to empathize with poor messaging, when in fact, the "white space" creates it.

To eradicate poor messaging and to be assured that misrepresentation is the result of human error rather than racial degradation, society would have to do a complete renovation to itself. Currently, every facet of society needs equal representation and voice at the table, and yet efforts to ensure this is quite minimal.

Black women (professional, educated, and phenomenal), when you are seated at the table, but you do not contribute your ideas, or you are gray, because you do not love the essence of who you are, why are you sitting at the table at all? Your experience is invaluable, and your knowledge is profound. You must impart it, and sharpen one another with it.

On the other hand, if you do not have a seat at the table, and decisions are made that impact you, you must hold those seated at the table accountable for creating obstacles that omit you from having the opportunity to contribute.

Organize and come together to build one another with enlightenment and strategy. Your strategizing could potentially gain a highly qualified Black, professional, educated woman access to an arena that has systemically overlooked her. Black women, allow your character to embolden you to produce your own opportunities thereby creating opportunity for others.

Truly, we must establish our own brands in all institutions if we want to see our truest potential. However, in the meantime, the society we live in, which constitutes the "white space", must be willing to eliminate its blind-spots, and if it remains unwilling, *we* must be willing to do it ourselves.

CHAPTER 11

The Black Text is Necessary

A Writer's "white space"

We are all authors whether we have published any of our writings or not; it is our stories that manifest as experiences, which create the Black text. It is our unique experiences that shape how we socialize with the world around us. It is our responsibility to listen more and to speak less.

When we listen, we can start to appreciate the stories of others, and in doing so, we can begin to see a deeper and ever so obvious truth that not one person's experience is the same – despite our most superficial similarities: gender, sexual orientation, and race. By hearing from one another, we learn from each other how the circumstances in our narratives are constantly shaping us into the people we are intended to be.

We were created to live as a collective body; we were created to be empathetic. Empathy is engendered in connecting with another so deeply we can feel their joy, their sadness, their pain, and their struggles as if it is real to us. However, it is the systemic process of societal normalization that has programed humanity into creating enclaves around our similarities, which have isolated our innate desire to discover and appreciate the unique social experiences around us. Our isolation has created discrimination and classism, because our ego struggles to honor the contribution of and connection to others.

We collectively allow the "white space" to oppress us, while each represented group declares, "My race is better than yours; my gender is better than yours; my pockets are fuller than yours." In speaking these ideas of superiority, we continue to perpetuate the practice of isolation and degradation that does not contribute to society, but rather, it handicaps it.

We should see ourselves in the same way we look at constructing a message. To create a single thought, we need the essential parts of a sentence: the complete subject, the complete predicate, and the ending punctuation. Each element is necessary in order to express an idea. At some point, we must begin to be pure-hearted enough to earnestly share this blank space with Black text.

Nonetheless, inquiring minds would like to know. If a writer's "white space" causes writer's block, what does society's "white space" cause?

A Word of Advice

Keep a daily diary of your experiences at work, because writing can be quite therapeutic. While it is therapeutic, reflecting on your written experience can help you to evaluate your responses to the scenarios you encounter within the "white space". Once you have journaled your experience, read it objectively. In other words, read it without your strongest emotion. Be bipartisan.

Reflect and determine if what you have experienced could have been avoided, and if so, determine what you could have done differently. However, if what you have experienced could not have been avoided, determine why. If you had a response, judge it. Was it concise? Was it professional? Did it send a message that you mean business?

If you did not respond, determine why. If you did not know how to respond, identify the antagonist, identify the conflict, and write down several responses for the scenario that concurrently prove to be concise, professional, and unemotional.

By all means, just write. Write, because it is a way to fill in the "white spaces" with Black ink. Black ink that has a narrative worthy to be shared and appreciated. Write, because it allows for your strongest emotions to be released as a result of the attempts of oppression within the "white space" that you, Black, professional, educated woman, have stored up within your subconscious.

Write, because it will force you to notice, plan for, and address the passive attempts to minimize your contribution; it will allow for you to dispel the idea of a so-called "white space", and your sophistication will permeate a freshness that recreates spaces. Write, because another Black, professional, educated woman has had or will have the same experience as you, so mentor the sister you have never met with your words of wisdom, because she needs you. So, *write*.

CHAPTER 12

Point-Blank Period.

She is here…

There is no secret that Black women have been diligent in earning advanced degrees, which qualifies her for prestigious professional opportunities. However, if Black women are not being overlooked to less qualified white candidates or if she earns the candidacy, she must inevitably experience the passive attempts to oppress her magnanimous strength and competence.

It is the small – seemingly insignificant moments that she notices are attempts to stifle her purposeful existence in the spaces that are so blessed to have her. At least once every other week, she and her white colleague of equal title, but not so equal education or experience, will invariably stand or sit beside one another when a white stakeholder approaches them with an inquiry resting at the tip of the tongue.

To the white stakeholder, she is invisible, while her white colleague is a radiant ray of existence. She already knows what to expect, so she remains beside her white colleague, and she watches the eyes. It is the same song and dance – a waltz between two pairs of eyeballs over Gomersall's "Blue Skies."

She witnesses the white stakeholder, a stranger to both she and her white colleague, establish a rapport grounded in an arrogant sameness. The white stakeholder

127

asks the question directly with a certain level of esteem and confidence in the capacity of the white face at the other end of it, and she notices her white colleague's oppressive attempt to block her out with a subtle repositioning of the body.

Her white colleague and this white stakeholder literally create a "white space" right before her eyes. Enlivened, her white colleague puts a series of words together in hopes that it lands on something that is coherent, and the white stakeholder, in an attempt to respect the whiteness while a Black face is within ear and eyeshot, feigns understanding of the gibberish.

As if to pay homage to the indigenous people, she reclaims her space with an equally subtle repositioning, and to clarify a misnomer her white colleague just offered the white stakeholder, she nonchalantly makes room for herself. Though she offers an unobjectionable truth, the white stakeholder looks at her Black face with a quivered lip and pierced gaze – ears red with agitation, and a face that reads, "How dare you inform *me* of *a-n-y* thing?"

The white stakeholder decides that it is better to make this Black face invisible once more, and thereby removes the focused gaze from the Black face to repositions it upon the white – an action that represents the psychological ramifications; that the white stakeholder reserves deference to the misinformation of another white face over the disdain for the accuracy of a Black one.

A Word of Advice

Speak your truth, but do so without the emotion that is boiling up within you. Do not allow anyone to white you out of a space to which you are entitled to exist and to contribute. In the case of the persona referred to as "she", the attempts to muffle her presence was a collaborative effort that many white people do when they out number Black, professional, educated women.

However, "she" casually made her presence known, when she repositioned herself in response to their attempts to spatially ostracize her. "She" also coolly commanded respect when she provided accurate information to her white colleague's misinformation.

Her goal was not to change the mindset of her white colleague nor the white stakeholder; however, her goal was to assert that she understands the passive aggressive game they were compelled to play because of her race and gender, and she affirmed that she is stars and moons above it.

CONCLUSION

Now What?

A Black woman's psychological jujitsu

J ui Jitsu is explained as a method developed in Japan It is the art of defending oneself without the use of weapons by using the strength and weight of an adversary to disable him. Hence, a Black woman's psychological jujitsu is required in the "white space". She must protect herself from the existing paradigm – that being the "white shade" she experiences in the "white space", but she must do so by removing emotion that will only fuel a misstep on her part.

Instead, she must use the "shader's" words and actions as a way to disarm him or her. She must be an allegorical mirror – hold it up to the "shader", because by doing so, she is informing them of her awareness of their intentions, while concurrently forcing them to confront it themselves. Nonetheless, it is not the Black, professional, educated woman's job to inspire a change of heart in the "shader", it is merely her duty to subtly expose it.

Black women must accept the fact that we will inevitably experience "white shade" in the "white space", and the lack of preparation is where our failure lies, and it must be noted that our power lies in our collective awareness and response.

From this time forward, I endow a Black woman's psychological jujitsu as an official art form, so please use the stories and the advice I offer in this text to indoctrinate you.

A Tri-Meaning: "white space"

There are (3) versions of the "white space" that prove to be relevant to this text. The first explains the marketing term, which is essentially an omission of a marketing perspective.

In a cultural society, this omission could be detrimental if and when the forgotten or incorrectly represented perspective is prejudice in any way. Such a power structure exists through a lack, false, or exaggerated representation.

The second version of the "white space" discusses a writer's perspective; it is where a story begins. Everyone has a story, and so an untold story only creates "white space".

Finally, the third and key definition extends the societal perspective of the marketing term. It is the unspoken, but known privileges of the majority. It is their domineering position in society and the direct impact it has on Black people that is oftentimes minimized.

However, the "white space" is a virus. These are metaphorical stories that belong to real people that have truly been infected by it. The stories of the impoverish and uneducated are all the world know, but for many Black people, there is a story of the inherent racism that manifests in professional and educational contexts that go untold.

Definition #1:

Harvard Business Review published an article by Mark W. Johnson entitled, "Where Is Your White Space." Johnson discusses the ambiguity of the term "white space" within the business world, and notes, "Some people define it as a place where there's no competition. Others as an entirely new market."

Johnson writes, "I suggest that it's more productive to view it as an internal signpost — as a way to map your company's ability to address new opportunities or threats. So, by 'white space', I mean 'market opportunities your company may wish — or need — to pursue that it cannot address unless it develops a new business model.'"

When Johnson asserts a "need" to pursue, the "need" is often a missing perspective. Therefore, it can be inferred that his advice serves as instruction for businesses to identify that missing element and include it in an effort to create a more accurate depiction.

Furthermore, the ideas that you have read in this text are driven by this definition. It is imperative that readers understand that this text is from the perspective of a Black, professional, educated woman, and that the four identifying characteristics must be linked in order to appreciate the relevance of this text. It must be noted that the experience of a Black, professional, educated woman has depth; however, her experience is often missing in the spaces she occupies.

Oftentimes, it is intentionally ignored, blurred, skewed, or deemed irrelevant.

Definition #2:

Alexa Gilker, a screenwriter and playwright has a website called *Whitespace Writers*. Within the site's "About" page, there is a compelling and unique explanation for the term "white space", and it indirectly ties with the previous definition. It states:

> "White space" is a term typically used in
> graphic design to literally mean the white
> space on a page, or the spaces between the
> images or words. For our purpose as writers,
> however, we steal (like all good writers do)
> the term "white space" to mean "the place
> where storytelling happens beyond the
> words."

And so, as you have read this text, my hope is that you have come to appreciate the experience of the Black, professional, educated women you encounter. It is important that the reader understands that each story is merely a moment in her life; she lives the experience daily. Also, these stories not only fill the "white space" of these pages, but hopefully resonated with you so deeply that your understanding of these women will elicit a trust and compassion for her truth, because she deserves it.

Definition #3:

American Sociological Association extracted and published "The White Space" by Elijah Anderson from his larger text *Race Space, Integration, and Inclusion?* Anderson's abstract synthesizes the racial truth behind the various meanings of the term – "white space". It states:

> Since the end of the Civil Rights Movement,
> large numbers of Black people have made

their way into settings previously occupied by whites, though their reception has been mixed. Overwhelmingly, white neighborhoods, schools, workplaces, restaurants, and other public spaces remain. Blacks perceive such settings as "the white space," which they often consider to be informally "off limits" for people like them.

Anderson's abstract goes on to say:

> Despite the growth of an enormous Black middle class, many whites assume that the natural Black space is that destitute and fearsome locality so commonly featured in the public media, including popular books, music and videos, and the TV news – the iconic ghetto. White people typically avoid Black space[s], but Black people are required to

navigate the white space as a condition of
their existence.

It is this third definition that ties the intention of this text.

It is my duty as a Black, professional, educated woman to bring to light the injustices of being born into a condition that is out of my direct control, while concurrently existing within its confines. It is my responsibility (and the responsibility of others) to eradicate this ideology.

However, the task will not be without challenge, because to attempt to eradicate it is a direct attack at the comfort of those who dominate societal norms through the justice system, through the media, through the literature, and through all other bureaucracies. These settings are all examples of the "white space".

For now, this text is a start, and I hope that you have enjoyed these vignettes told in the form of parable, caricature, and truth.

References

Anderson, E. (2014.). The White
Space. *American Sociological Association*. Retrieved
from
https://sociology.yale.edu/sites/default/files/pages_fro
m_sre-11_rev5_printer_files.pdf

Dove. 2009. Unilever. 21 Feb 2009. http://www.Dove.com

Failure Is Not An Option For Black Women: Effects Of
Organizational Performance On Leaders With Single
Versus Dual-Subordinate Identities. (n.d.). Retrieved
from   https://gap.hks.harvard.edu/failure-not-option-
black-women-effects-organizational-performance-
leaders-single-versus-dual

Froehlich, K. (n.d.). *Dove: Changing the Face of Beauty?*

Gilker, A. (n.d.). Whitespace Writers. Retrieved
from http://www.whitespacewriters.com

Hess, C., Lacarte, V., & Hegewisch, A. (2019, September 11).
Pay Equity & Discrimination. *Institution for Women's
Policy   Research*.   Retrieved   from
https://iwpr.org/issue/employment-education-
economic-change/pay-equity-discrimination/

Johnson, M. W. (2012). Where Is Your White Space? *Harvard
Business Review*. Retrieved from
https://hbr.org/2010/02/where-is-your-white-space

Johnson, Olivia. "How Dove Changed the Rules of the Beauty
Game." Market Leader. 31 2005:

43-6. Business Source Complete. EBSCO. 22 March 2009 http://web.ebscohost.com/bsi/search

Samuel Osborne @SamuelOsborne93. (2016, June 3). Black women become most educated group in US. Retrieved from https://www.independent.co.uk/news/world/americas/black-women-become-most-educated-group-in-us-a7063361.html

Thompson, S. (2019, August 22). Despite Being the Most Educated, Black Women Earn Less Money at Work, in Entrepreneurship, and in Venture Capital. 3 Ways to Fix It. Retrieved from https://www.inc.com/sonia-thompson/black-women-equal-pay-equity-how-to-make-progress.html

Zen, O. (2019). How Dove's Real Beauty campaign won, and nearly lost, its audience. *PR Week*. Retrieved from https://www.prweek.com/article/1582147/doves-real-beauty-campaign-won-nearly-lost-its-audience